BULBS IN BLOOM

BULBS IN BLOOM

BULBS, CORMS, TUBERS, RHIZOMES, AND TUBEROUS ROOTS

PETER ARNOLD

LAUREL
GLEN

PUBLISHED AND PRODUCED IN THE UNITED STATES BY

LAUREL GLEN PUBLISHING
5880 OBERLIN DRIVE, SUITE 400
SAN DIEGO, CA 92121-4794
http://www.advantagebooksonline.com

Arnold, Peter, 1946-
    Bulbs in bloom : Bulbs, Corms, Tubers, Rhizomes, and Tuberous Roots/Peter Arnold.
        p.   cm.
    Includes index.
    ISBN 1-57145-645-7
    1. Bulbs. 2. Bulbs Pictorial works. I. Title.
    SB425.A74   1999   99-42673
    635.9'4'0222—dc21   CIP

                    1 2 3 4 5 99 00 01 02 03

                    PUBLISHER: ALLEN ORSO
                MANAGING EDITOR: JOANN PADGETT
                ASSOCIATE EDITOR: ELIZABETH MCNULTY
            COVER AND INTERIOR DESIGNER: NIGEL PARTRIDGE
                COLOR ART DIRECTOR: RICHARD RUNYON
                LINE ILLUSTRATIONS: ELIZABETH DOWLE

            PRINTED IN CHINA BY PALACE PRESS INTERNATIONAL.

HALF-TITLE: *COLCHICUM SPECIOSUM* (AUTUMN CROCUS)
FRONTISPIECE: *CROCUS* 'VERNUS WHITE'
TITLE PAGE: *CYCLAMEN*
DEDICATION PAGE: *POLYGONATUM* X HYBRIDUM (SOLOMON'S SEAL)

CONTENTS

DEDICATION
Especially for Prapan Phaiwongse
"Be brave, embrace the world, and do not be afraid of change."

ACKNOWLEDGMENTS
Peter Arnold would like to thank Allen Orso and JoAnn Padgett, Elizabeth Dowle for her beautiful illustrations, Nigel Partridge for his design input and patience, and Gerald Grant and Linsdey Western for their help with the text. Thanks to everyone associated with the production of both the images and the book, not only for their kind help but also for their enthusiastic cooperation.

I would also like to acknowledge my extended family: Sybil, Kay and Rick Runyon, Jean, Barbara, Khun Dam, Suchart Lakdee, Chito, Betsy and Maurice, and Roberto Maramba and Irene Maag, for their encouragement and support.

FOREWORD

Following the sellout successes of my books *Orchids* and *Tulips*, my publishers waited eagerly for a follow-up. At first I toyed with various possibilities: lilies, dahlias, irises, or a collection of spring flowers. Suddenly it dawned on me that most of the flowers I was contemplating fell under the category of "bulbous plants." What a wonderful solution to bring together so many of my favorite flowers! And that is how *Bulbs in Bloom* was conceived.

My fondness for flowering bulbs dates back to childhood when, during the first dark evenings of the year, my mother encouraged my three sisters and me to rummage through bulb catalogs and choose a selection for planting in the garden borders. A few select bulbs were also chosen for planting in containers and would produce a marvelous and colorful show of spring cheer in the house during the months of January and February when English skies are at their grayest.

My sisters always chose simple pastel-colored blooms. I went for the more exotic: the frilled and feathered tulips, the double hyacinths, and the multiheaded or double-petaled narcissus. We were never disappointed with the results of our endeavors. During the worst days of winter we enjoyed first the vibrant colors of daffodils, next tulips, and then the heady scent of hyacinths wafting through the house.

April and May brought much admiration of our garden by guests and passersby. As we grew older, and our gardens extended to several acres, we bought lilies, gladiolus, dahlias, and later more exotic species such as amaryllis, begonias, and calla lilies. We have retained our great love of flowers throughout our lives.

As children, we soon forgot about the bulbs in the ground. Once they had flowered, the job of lifting and storing was left to our mother. Occasionally, a few random flowers brazenly bloomed amid the next year's display. Where the bulbs from the previous year had gone never seemed to concern us!

It wasn't until our early teens that we were taught the more laborious chore of digging up the bulbs and storing them for the summer. We neatly labeled them with colorful illustrated tags cut from old gardening magazines to identify the varieties and species for planning our new gardening scheme the following year.

In our childhood naiveté, they were all just bulbs. I'm sure that many of you have experienced the ease with which it is possible to bring bulbs into flower. At least for the first time, that is. We can all buy bulbs from our local garden center or nursery, plant them, and simply allow nature to take over. But to bring those same bulbs into flower year after year requires a little extra knowledge and work.

There are, of course, bulbous plants that flower throughout the different seasons of the year. Plan your planting well and you will have yearlong color in the garden. To me, the joy of snowdrops and crocuses pushing their way up through the snows of late winter herald the coming of spring. Other bulbs thrive in the hot summer sun, and others still bloom even through the last days of fall. Then there are the many varieties that have been specially cultivated to flower inside the house and to withstand central heating.

For this book I started the project by collecting flowering bulb catalogs and sifting through them for candidates to photograph. Initially my artist's eye focused on the image's impact, but as my research continued, I expanded my original choices to include more varied floral forms and colors. I have included old standards alongside the exotics, and bulbs to suit a variety of climates in America, Europe, and the tropics. Commercial availability of the featured bulbs was also given consideration.

Most of the bulbs were grown under controlled conditions, so as the seasons passed I was able to expand my photographic selection as they came into bloom. With the final stage of the book fast approaching, I photographed the remaining blooms for color, form, and texture to complement the layout.

My style of photography has been consistent throughout the years. I give special thought to the graphic composition and then consider the character, color, form, and texture of the particular flower being photographed. I compare this artistic process to photographing a beautiful model by closely studying her face and then deciding how to enhance the characteristics that make that face beautiful. I have attempted to capture the unique aesthetics of these extraordinary flowers in their moment of splendor.

The flowers are set against black, white, or neutral-toned backgrounds. The graphic form thus has more impact and the flower's characteristics are accentuated. The background color is not as important to me as the final image. The background is standardized so as not to detract from the flowers themselves.

Some blooms are photographed on location in natural light, while others are captured on film under artificial light in my studio. I use a semiportable electronic flash unit with a single flash-head light source to light the subject in conjunction with the black backgrounds. To achieve a white background in natural light, I place the subject in the shade and position the white paper backdrop so that it gets full sun, giving a one- or two-stop differential between the light on the background and the light on the subject. With artificial light in the studio, I either use an extra flash-head directed onto a white paper backdrop, giving a one-stop differential, or backlight through opaque Plexiglas. When needed, I use a reflective card to direct light into the shadowy areas of the center of the flower or to the underside of the petals.

My camera is a rather ancient Hasselblad 500 CM that I bought in my early days of photography. I usually use either an 80mm or 150mm Sonar lens, sometimes in conjunction with extension tubes or proxars for very close-up or macro shots.

Most of my photographs were exposed at aperture f.22 or f.32 to give optimum depth of field and sharpness to the images. I usually bracket my exposures half an f-stop on each side of the metered light reading to obtain precise color rendition and perfect exposure.

I use Fuji and Kodak film. My exhibition prints and signed limited-edition prints are made on Ilfordchrome classic paper and Fuji ultragloss paper.

Some of my photographs were taken in England and on location in Europe and the United States. Others were taken in Thailand, where I have a second home. I researched and wrote most of the text on location in Thailand, where I am sponsoring the building of a school for orphans, very poor children, and children infected with the HIV virus. Ten percent of my proceeds from the sale of this book will go directly to the school and the welfare of those children.

INTRODUCTION

Everyone is familiar with the bright colors of cultivated flowering bulbs grown in springtime, but we must not forget the more subtle beauty of their natural counterparts found in the countryside and woodlands. These familiar species include common snowdrops, winter aconites, bluebells, and windflowers.

The dainty snowdrops come first, often pushing their way through the snow. Crocuses follow and later daffodils, hyacinths, grape hyacinth, and then tulips. These striking flowers are popular bulbs for both large and small home gardens, as well as for displays in parks and public places. Many bulbs have been cultivated specifically for indoor displays; others are cultivated especially for the cut flower industry. Bulbous plants are truly versatile.

Bulbs provide flowers of an infinite variation of color, shape, size, and texture, and it is with this in mind that I have chosen the following photographic portfolio. Generally, the term "bulb" is used very loosely and is accepted as the name for a wide variety of plants. In fact it is not botanically correct for many species, of which only half are true bulbs; the others are corms, tubers, rhizomes, or tuberous roots. Bulb suppliers have grouped them together for convenience. However, they do have one thing in common; they all have developed underground storage systems. Recently the term "geophyte" has been introduced to refer collectively to herbaceous perennials with fleshy underground structures, the primary function of which is to store food and moisture.

Over millions of years of evolution, plants have found ingenious ways to survive. Most bulbs originate from areas where the adverse environment enforces a period of dormancy, either due to intense cold or frost, but also often due to very hot and extremely dry summer periods. The bulb survives through photosynthesis by gathering nutrients through its leaves. Nutrients are stored in the underground bulb system during the normal growth period. This allows the plant to remain dormant during unfavorable weather and to wait for better conditions the next season for regrowth.

Today there are about three thousand species of bulbs, and after many years of cultivation and crossbreeding, varieties have been developed that will flower in almost any part of the world.

TRUE BULBS

The true bulb is a swollen, dormant underground stem base that encompasses a complete or nearly complete embryonic plant with leaves, stem, and flower bud. Modified leaves or "scales" overlap one another to surround and protect this embryonic plant. These scales may be thin and tightly layered, as in the case of the tulip and daffodil, or fleshy and loosely layered, as in the case of the lily. The scales contain stores of reserve food including sugar, starch, and various proteins. Usually true bulbs have a swollen, pear-shaped appearance. At the base of the bulb is a disk of hardened stem tissue called the "basal plate," which holds the base of scales together and is the point from which the roots emerge at the beginning of a new growth cycle.

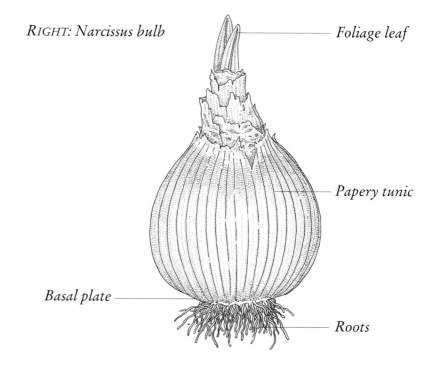

RIGHT: Narcissus bulb

Foliage leaf

Papery tunic

Basal plate

Roots

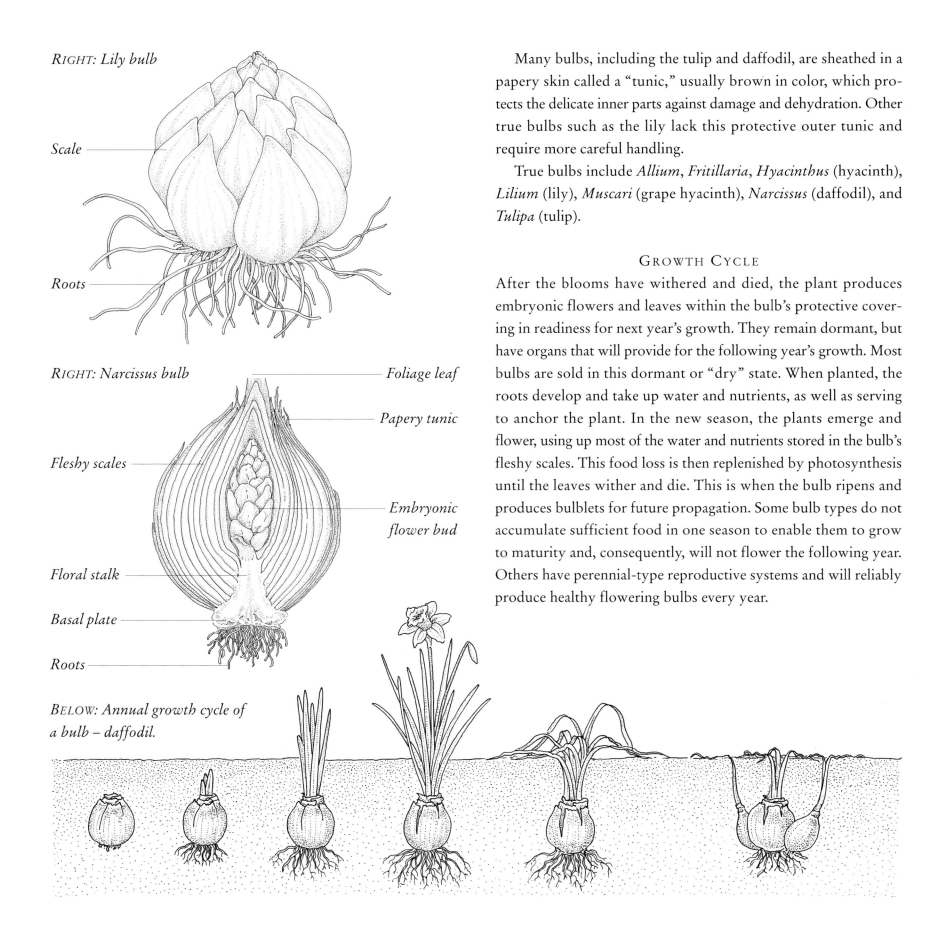

RIGHT: Lily bulb

Scale

Roots

RIGHT: Narcissus bulb

Foliage leaf

Papery tunic

Fleshy scales

Embryonic
flower bud

Floral stalk

Basal plate

Roots

*BELOW: Annual growth cycle of
a bulb – daffodil.*

Many bulbs, including the tulip and daffodil, are sheathed in a papery skin called a "tunic," usually brown in color, which protects the delicate inner parts against damage and dehydration. Other true bulbs such as the lily lack this protective outer tunic and require more careful handling.

True bulbs include *Allium*, *Fritillaria*, *Hyacinthus* (hyacinth), *Lilium* (lily), *Muscari* (grape hyacinth), *Narcissus* (daffodil), and *Tulipa* (tulip).

GROWTH CYCLE

After the blooms have withered and died, the plant produces embryonic flowers and leaves within the bulb's protective covering in readiness for next year's growth. They remain dormant, but have organs that will provide for the following year's growth. Most bulbs are sold in this dormant or "dry" state. When planted, the roots develop and take up water and nutrients, as well as serving to anchor the plant. In the new season, the plants emerge and flower, using up most of the water and nutrients stored in the bulb's fleshy scales. This food loss is then replenished by photosynthesis until the leaves wither and die. This is when the bulb ripens and produces bulblets for future propagation. Some bulb types do not accumulate sufficient food in one season to enable them to grow to maturity and, consequently, will not flower the following year. Others have perennial-type reproductive systems and will reliably produce healthy flowering bulbs every year.

CORMS

Corms often look like true bulbs. They are usually round in appearance like the crocus corm, but others tend to be flattened at the top as in the case of the gladiolus corm. Made up of the base of a plant stem that has swollen to become an underground storage system, corms differ from true bulbs in that the solid mass is made of "bulb" tissue rather than from a series of overlapping modified scales. Corms are predominantly comprised of basal plate tissue rather than scale tissue; the basal plate contains most of the nutrient reserves.

At the start of the growth cycle, roots emerge from the basal plate at the corm's base. Shoots develop from the top of the corm. Like bulbs, corms are often covered in a tunic of papery skin. However, this is formed from the dried bases of the previous year's leaf growth rather than the scales. When purchasing, make sure that the tunic is intact.

All corms reproduce by annual replacement. Each year the plant's growth and flowering process depletes the stored nutrients. As the corm shrinks at the end of the growth cycle, one or more new corms are formed from buds that appear at the top or on the side of the old corm. Small "offsets" called "cormels" are often produced around the new corm's base.

Crocus, Freesia, Gladiolus, Ixia (African corn lily), *Sparaxis* (velvet flower), and *Watsonia* (bugle lily) are typical corms.

BELOW: Annual growth cycle of a corm – gladiolus.

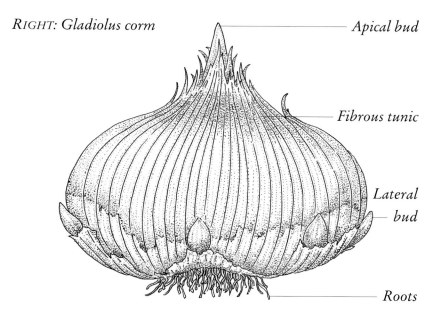

RIGHT: Gladiolus corm

Apical bud

Fibrous tunic

Lateral bud

Roots

TUBERS

Tubers are easily distinguishable from bulbs and corms by the absence of a tunic. Tubers are still derived from enlarged stem tissue that has formed an underground store of nutrients, but they have no basal plate. They don't have an organized structure and can be cylindrical or flattened, or oddly shaped and plump with a knobby surface on the side and base and sometimes on the top as well. Tubers have multiple growth points, or "eyes," on their upper surface from which shoots emerge to produce new plants. These growth points are scale-like leaves with growth buds in the axis.

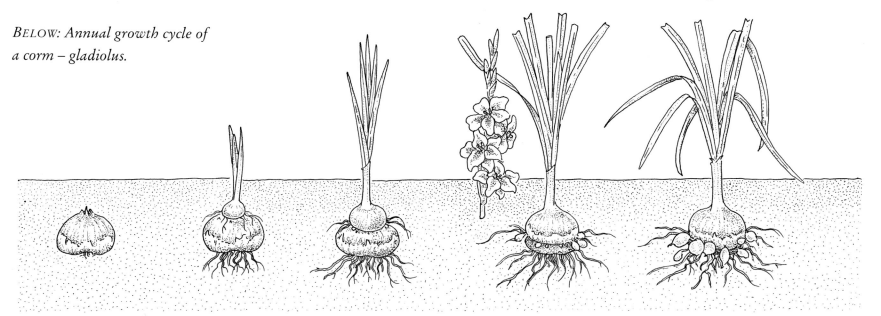

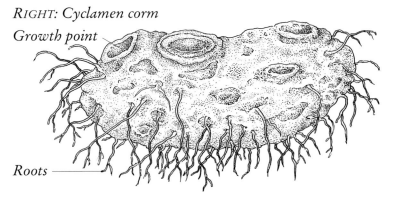

RIGHT: Cyclamen corm

Growth point

Roots

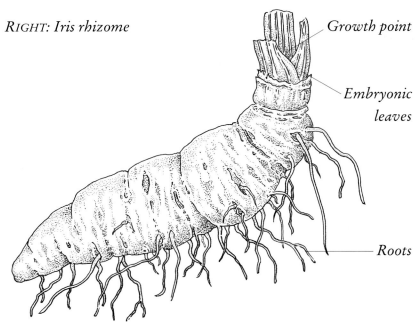

RIGHT: Iris rhizome

Growth point

Embryonic leaves

Roots

Some tubers, such as begonias, have a tendency to increase in size as they store nutrients. These tend not to produce new tubers. Others like the caladium produce protuberances that grow from the sides of the mother tuber. These can be removed and planted separately. Individual tubers can last for a number of years, increasing in size each year during vegetative growth. Care must be taken when handling tubers so as not to damage the "eyes" from which the shoots normally form.

Typical tubers are *Anemone* (windflower), *Arum* (calla lily), *Begonia*, *Cyclamen*, *Gloriosa*, and *Gloxinia*.

RHIZOMES

Rhizomes, corms, and tubers are all bulbous systems that are thickened stems filled with nutrients to support the new plant. Rhizomes are sometimes called rootstock. They have no basal plate and no tunic. They characteristically grow horizontally, either partially under the soil surface or sometimes across the surface. The primary growing point is at the tip of the rhizome, encased in scale-like embryonic leaves. As the rhizome creeps across the soil, it sends out shoots that grow into mature plants. Growth buds with small leaves also form along the upper surface and along the sides. Roots develop from buds along the underside of the rhizome. Each year, during the vegetative period, the rhizome develops new protuberances, thus increasing its size.

BELOW: Annual growth cycle of a tuber – begonia.

Cutting the horizontal stem into segments for planting can easily propagate most rhizomes. Care must be taken to make sure that each section has roots and at least one bud. Lily of the valley bears upright growths known as "pips," which can be detached and stored for planting later.

Among the best-known rhizomatous plants are *Agapanthus* (lily of the Nile), *Iris* x *germanica* (bearded iris), and *Zantedeschia* (calla lily).

TUBEROUS ROOTS

Although all bulbs grow underground, the tuberous root is actually the only true root. It differs from the others by being a swollen root instead of a swollen stem or collection of scale leaves. Tuberous roots are thickened fleshy roots rather than modified stem bases, and their nutrient supply is contained in root tissue, not in stem or leaf tissue as in other bulbous systems. They are also called "root tubers" or tuber-like roots. They do not take in water but depend on their system of fibrous roots to take in moisture and nutrients from the soil.

Like tubers, tuberous roots produce growth buds from which new plants grow. However, these buds are usually found at the neck of the root at the base of the old stem. This upper section is usually called the "crown." Tuberous roots grow larger during the vegetative period and can be a single structure or branched in a clus-

RIGHT: Dahlia tuberous root

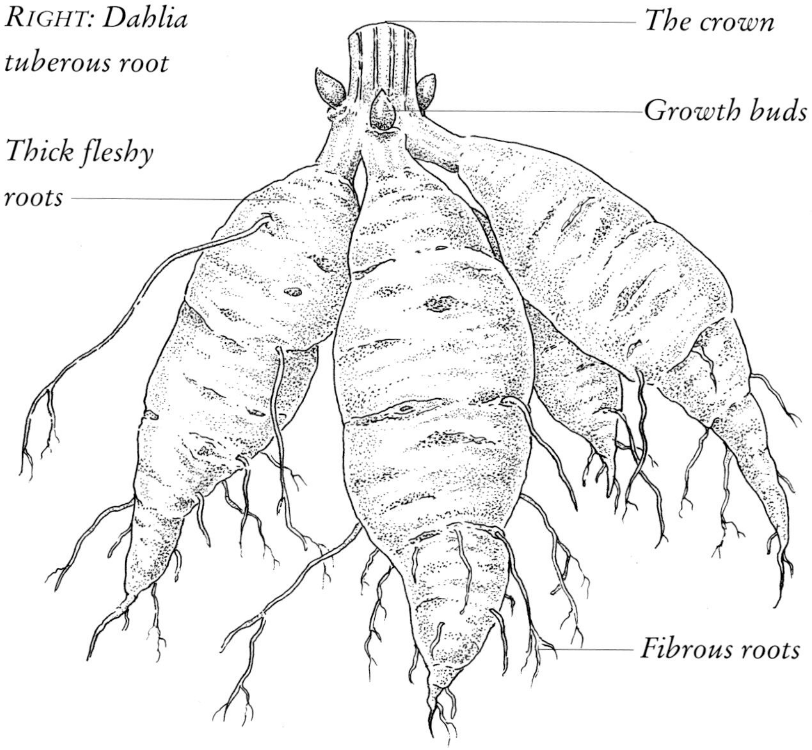

The crown

Growth buds

Thick fleshy roots

Fibrous roots

BELOW: Annual growth cycle of a rhizome – iris.

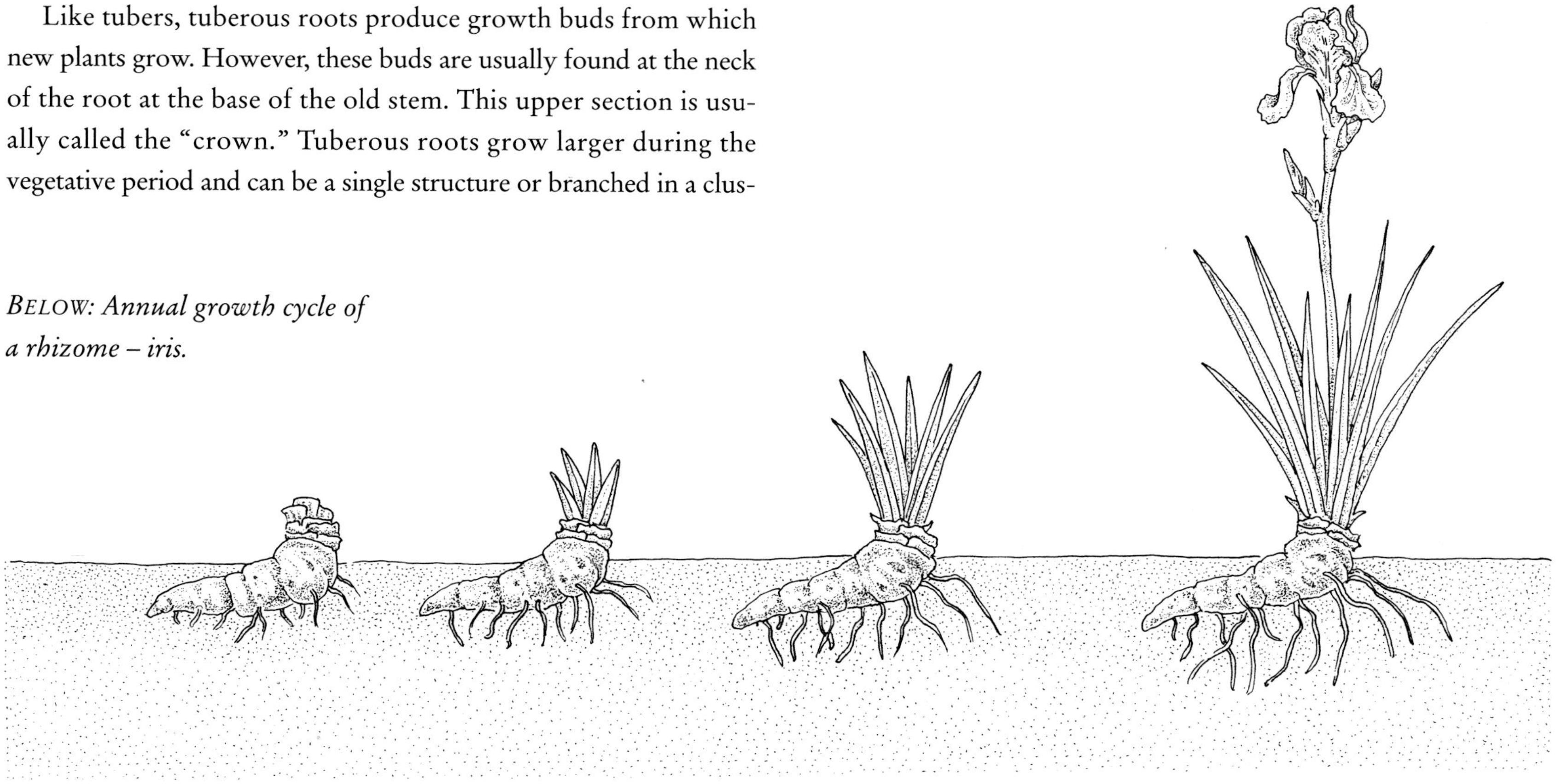

RIGHT: Cattleya *orchid*

ter. The dahlia has swollen tuberous roots radiating out from a central point. Each tuberous root can be separated to propagate another plant, but it is important to make sure that each has a growth bud or eye-bearing section at the top.

Typical tuberous roots are *Clivia* (Kaffir lily), *Dahlia*, *Eremurus* (foxtail lily), and *Ranunculus*.

PSEUDOBULBS AND STORAGE ROOTS

Certain orchids have developed in their own fascinating way to incorporate traits of bulbous plants. Some species have developed pseudobulbs which are thickened stem bases full of nutrients. From these pseudobulbs emerge new shoots, including both leaves and flowers. The *Pleione* is very like a true bulb that grows in the ground, while the cattleya family extends in a horizontal manner like a rhizome, but is usually anchored on a tree.

For comparison, I have also included photographs of a few flowers whose stems or roots thicken to store water and nutrients, even though they are not considered bulbous plants.

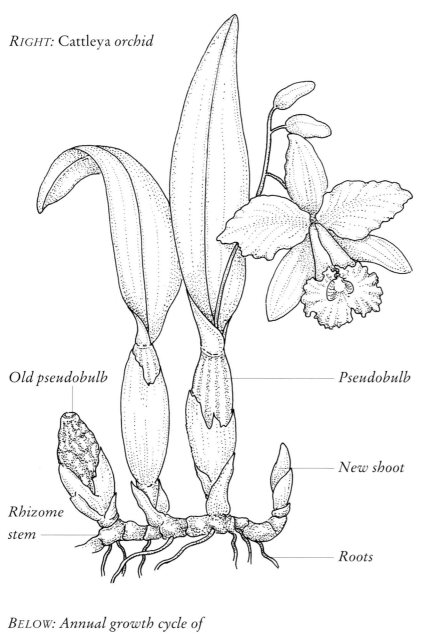

RIGHT: Cattleya *orchid*

Old pseudobulb

Pseudobulb

New shoot

Rhizome stem

Roots

BELOW: Annual growth cycle of a tuberous root – dahlia.

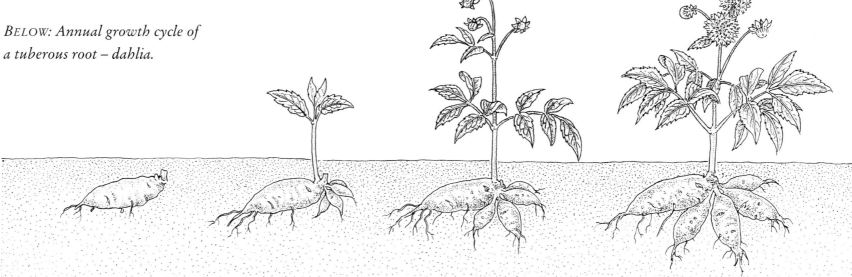

HISTORY

Interestingly, bulbs were probably some of the earliest plants ever cultivated. In prehistoric times, bulbous plants were eaten as a nutritious food source. Potatoes have been cultivated in South America for thousands of years, and onions were grown by the ancient Egyptians. During the Dark Ages in Europe, certain orchids were used as food and for medical treatments, and in the Near East, crocuses (*Crocus sativus*) were being grown for the saffron trade. Although many bulbs can be eaten, beware, many bulbs, such as *Convallaria* (lily of the valley), *Colchicum*, *Gloriosa*, *Leucojum*, and *Narcissus* are poisonous.

Inevitably, bulbs and bulbous flowers came to be valued as symbols. Madonna lilies were grown in Crete and Greece and are depicted on frescoes and decorative vases. These white lilies were greatly revered as a symbol of purity. In Christianity, they are symbolic of the Virgin Mary. In India and Egypt, the iris was held in esteem and is depicted in the frescoes and architecture. In France, the fleur-de-lis (iris) has been the symbol of the French kings since the fifth century.

During the fifteenth century, Arabs introduced bulbs into Europe, and it is well recorded that Suleiman "the Magnificent" of Turkey (1495–1566) was a great lover of gardens, and encouraged tulips and other bulbs to be widely grown. The tulip is one of the best-known bulbs and is often thought to have originated in Holland. But this is not so. The tulip and many other popular flowering bulbs are endemic to the mountainous foothills on both sides of the Mediterranean, through Asia Minor and Central Asia. The tulip's range also includes Iran, Afghanistan, Northern India, and China.

The first reference to tulips by a European dates from 1554 in a letter written by Ogier Ghiselin de Busbecq, the Viennese Ambassador to the Ottoman court of Sultan Suleiman the Magnificent. Busbecq described how, when traveling from Adrianople to Constantinople in Turkey "an abundance of flowers was every-

where offered to us—narcissus, hyacinth, and those which the Turks call *tulipam*, much to our wonderment, because of the time of year, it being almost the middle of winter, so unfriendly to flowers." Busbecq sent tulips and other bulbs from Turkey to Emperor Ferdinand I of Germany, who employed a botanist from the Netherlands known as Carolus Clusius. Clusius had been forced by a religious dispute to leave his homeland; he resettled in Germany as prefect of the royal medical gardens, where he received a large quantity of bulbs and seeds from Busbecq in 1573. He subsequently returned to Holland and was appointed professor of

RIGHT: Muscari

botany at Leiden, the university city on the Dutch coast. He became curator of the Hortus Botanical Gardens, which still exist today and are open to the public. Here Clusius experimented with bulb cultivation, and through his efforts, the Netherlands became the center of commercial bulb growing.

In England, flowering bulbs were recorded in John Gerard's famous herbal, published in 1597, and it is clear that bulb growing was well established by the early seventeenth century. Other publications including *Hortus Eystettensis* (1613) give an account of bulbs that were in cultivation at the time. There is also an account of the flowers grown in the garden of the Bishop of Eichstatt in central Germany by Crispin de Passe (*Hortus Floridus,* 1614) and later many are illustrated by John Parkinson (*Paradis in Sole,* 1629).

It was in 1623 that bulb growing began on a large scale. Because tulips and other bulbs were so well suited to formal garden displays, they rapidly gained popularity among the wealthy and fashionable classes of Austria, Germany, Flanders, and the Lowlands. In particular, enthusiasts were inspired to experiment with crossbreeding tulips, and many new and different varieties were produced. Demand forced prices up and soon created financial speculation, initially in France and then spreading northward through Flanders to Holland. Here the most astonishing drama in the history of horticulture happened: the phenomenon known as "Tulipmania" or "The Wind Trade." This extraordinary turn of events in Dutch history is well documented and developed from a particular characteristic of the tulip: its ability to diverge from the appearance of the mother plant, creating an interesting and colorful change of appearance. It is now known that this mutation is caused by a viral infection, but in the early days of bulb propagation it seemed to be a spontaneous phenomenon and captured the imagination of early admirers. Speculation in tulip bulbs reached its height between 1634 and 1636. Strange and novel forms of tulip flowers were much sought after, and they became a status symbol—a luxury that only the rich could afford. Tulip bulbs changed hands for completely unrealistic prices. There are records of a house being sold for three tulip bulbs. To stay in the market, people started to mortgage their homes and eventually speculative paper sales were made without the bulbs as assets. Inevitably this artificial market became saturated and, in February 1637, it crashed. Thousands were bankrupted. They lost their assets, and their lives were ruined. Tulipmania came to an abrupt end.

Bulbs have been grown in America from the earliest days of colonial settlement. European emigrants took seeds and bulbs to America in their personal luggage. More were sent for by the settlers once they had established themselves in their new country. Flowering bulbs are a common motif in paintings and domestic decorations dating from the seventeenth and eighteenth centuries. These were times of great adventure and discovery. The first major botanical expeditions were made to far corners of the earth including Australia, Japan, China, and the Caribbean. By the mid-eighteenth century, unusual plants never seen before were arriving in Europe and America.

With the Industrial Revolution taking place in Europe during the nineteenth century, certain flowering bulbs became cheaper, and the middle and lower classes were able to afford plants for their gardens. Farm laborers moved to the towns and began to miss the flowers of their countryside gardens. They turned to bulbs to decorate their gardens: tulips, anemone, hyacinth, and ranunculus. Cultivation and hybridization progressed in the commercial sector, but the more exotic plants continued to be sold only to the upper classes. Fortunately things changed with the coming of the twentieth century and flowers became affordable for everyone.

Bulb growing is now an important worldwide industry incorporating modern scientific technology. Demand for bulbs continues to increase each year. The United States has some important growing areas supplying its domestic bulb industry, although bulbs are still imported in great quantities directly from Holland. The Netherlands is still the world's leading producer of commercial bulbs. But it is surprising to learn that Great Britain comes second followed by the United States and Japan. As in Holland, the major bulb growing areas of the world have proved to be major tourist attractions, and more and more spring bulb festivals are held each year. See page 128 for a list of major international bulb festivals, displays, and celebrations.

THE PHOTOGRAPHS

1 *Allium* 'Globemaster'

2 *(left) Begonia* x *tuber hybrida*
'Double Picotee'

3 *(right) Lilium* 'Marco Polo'
(Lily)

4 *(left) Gloriosa superba* 'Rothschildiana'
(Flame lily, Glory lily)

5 *(above) Heliconia rostrata*

6 *(left) Arum creticum*
(Lords and Ladies)

7 *(right) Narcissus* 'Tête-à-tête'
(Daffodil)

9 *(above) Nymphaea capensis*
(Cape blue water lily)

10 *(below) Begonia pendula* 'Double pink'

11 *(right) Dahlia* 'Pearl of Heemstede'

14 *(left) Gladiolus* 'Chloe'
syn. *Acidanthera,* syn. *Homoglossum*

15 *(above) Iris* 'Chorus Girl'

16 *(below) Dicentra spectabilis f. alba*
(Bleeding heart, Lyre flower)

17 *(right) Convallaria majalis*
(Lily of the valley)

18 *(left) Ranunculus asiaticus* 'Champagne'
(Persian buttercup)

19 *(right) Cymbidium* 'Andre Ostobe'
(Orchid)

20 *(left) Tulipa* 'Balalaika'
(Tulip)

21 *(right) Nerine sarniensis*
(Guernsey lily)

23 *(above) Hermodactylus tuberosus,* syn. *Iris tuberosus*
(Widow iris, Snake's head iris)

24 *(below) Anthurium andraenum*
(Flamingo flower, Tail flower)

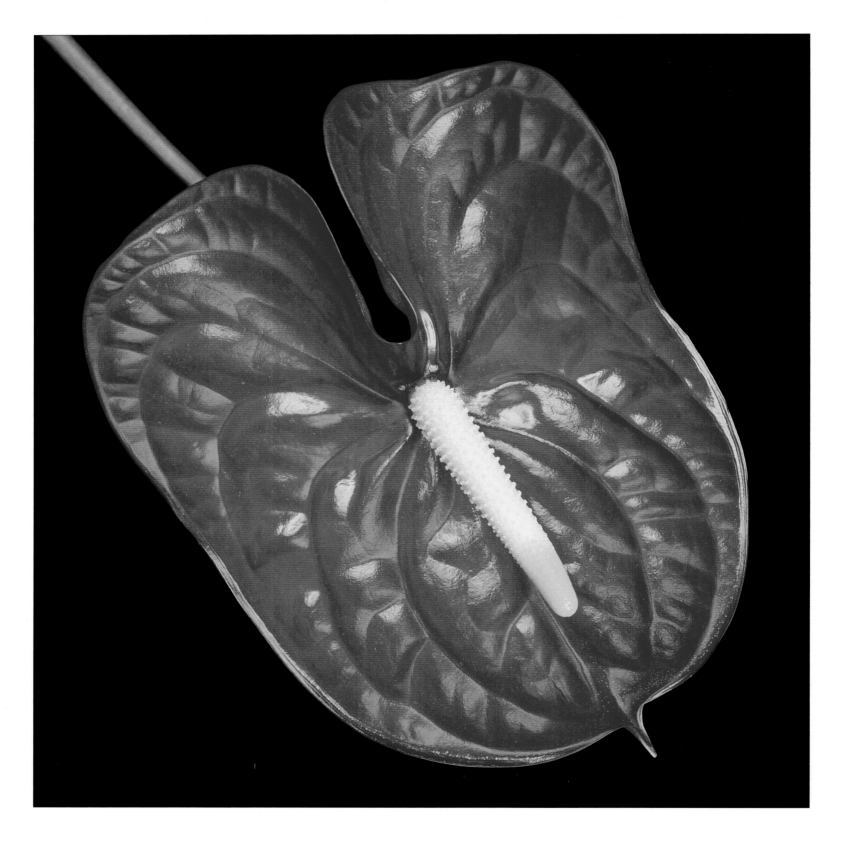

25 *(right) Crocosmia* 'Lucifer'
(Montbretia)

26 *(left) Hyacinthoides hispanica*
(Spanish bluebell)

27 *(above) Iris pallida*

28 *(left) Dodecatheon meadia alba*
(Shooting stars, American cowslip)

29 *(right) Zantedeschia aethiopica*
(Calla lily, Arum lily)

30 *(left) Hippeastrum*
'Blossom Peacock'
(Amaryllis)

31 *(right) Paeonia* 'Afterglow'
(Peony)

32 *(below)* *Hemerocallis* hybrid
(Daylily)

33 *(right)* *Kniphofia*
(Red-hot poker, Torch lily)

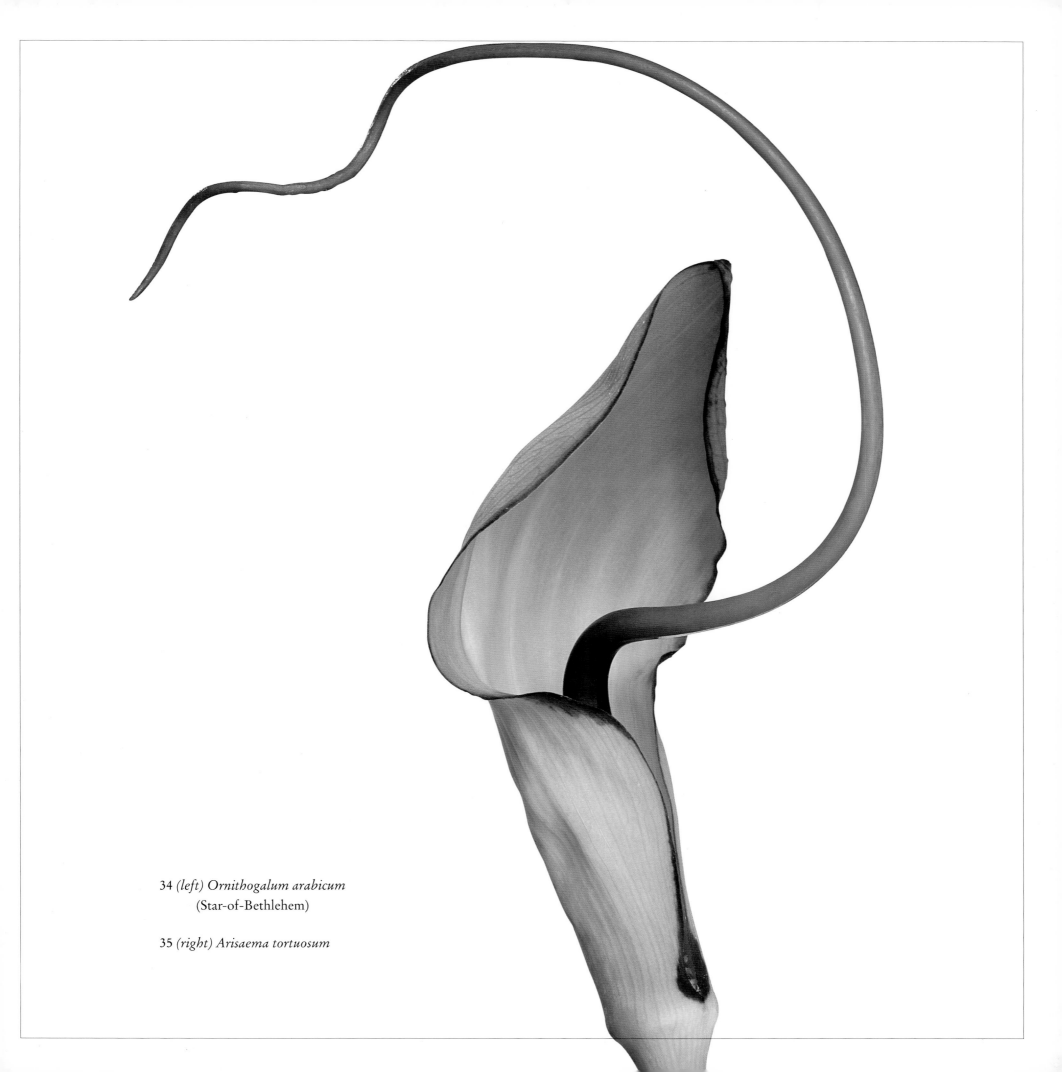

34 *(left) Ornithogalum arabicum*
(Star-of-Bethlehem)

35 *(right) Arisaema tortuosum*

36 *(below) Tulipa* 'Blue Parrot'
(Tulip)

37 *(right) Fritillaria meleagris*
(Checkered lily, Snake's head fritillary)

38 *(left) Trillium ovatum*
(Coast trillium)

39 *(right) Anemone blanda* 'White splendor'
(Grecian windflower)

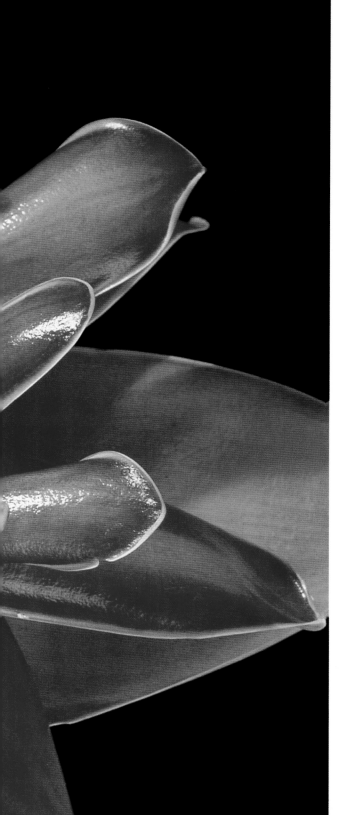

40 *(left) Etlingera elatior* syn. *Nicolaia elatior*
(Philippine waxflower, Torch ginger)

41 *(above) Anthurium scherzerianum* 'Rothschildianum'

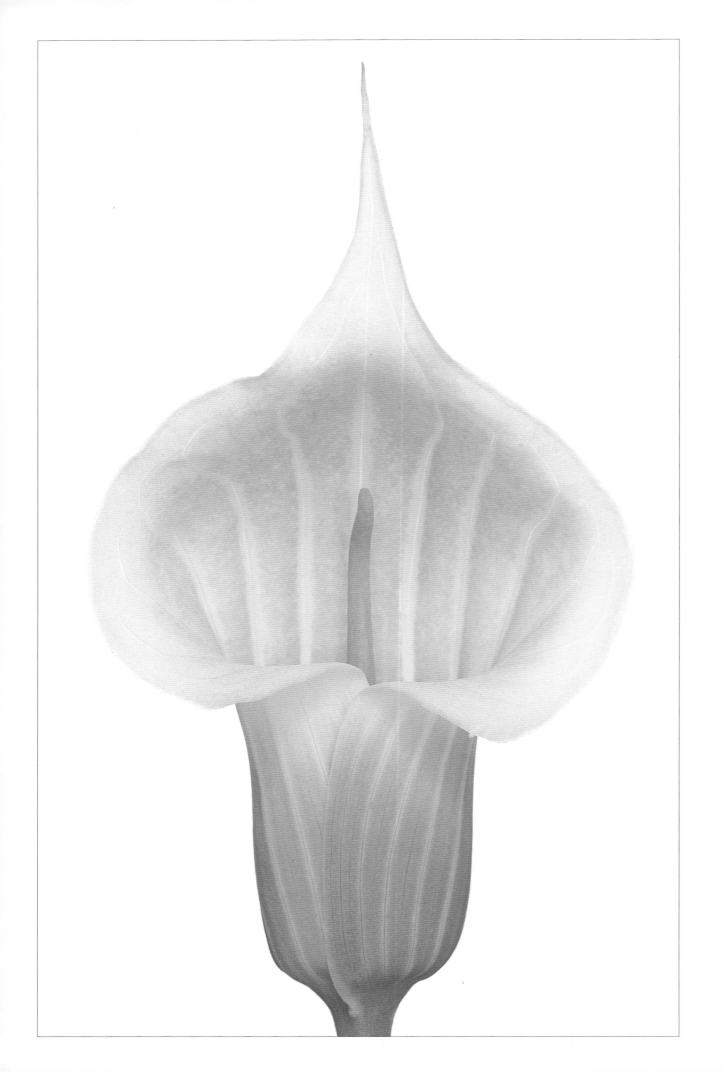

42 *(left) Arisaema candidissimum*

43 *(right) Lilium* 'Le Rêve'
(Lily)

44 *(overleaf) Muscari armeniacum*
(Grape hyacinth)

45 *(left) Dahlia* 'Trengrove Jill'

46 *(right) Lilium lancifolium*
syn. *L. tigrinum*
(Tiger lily)

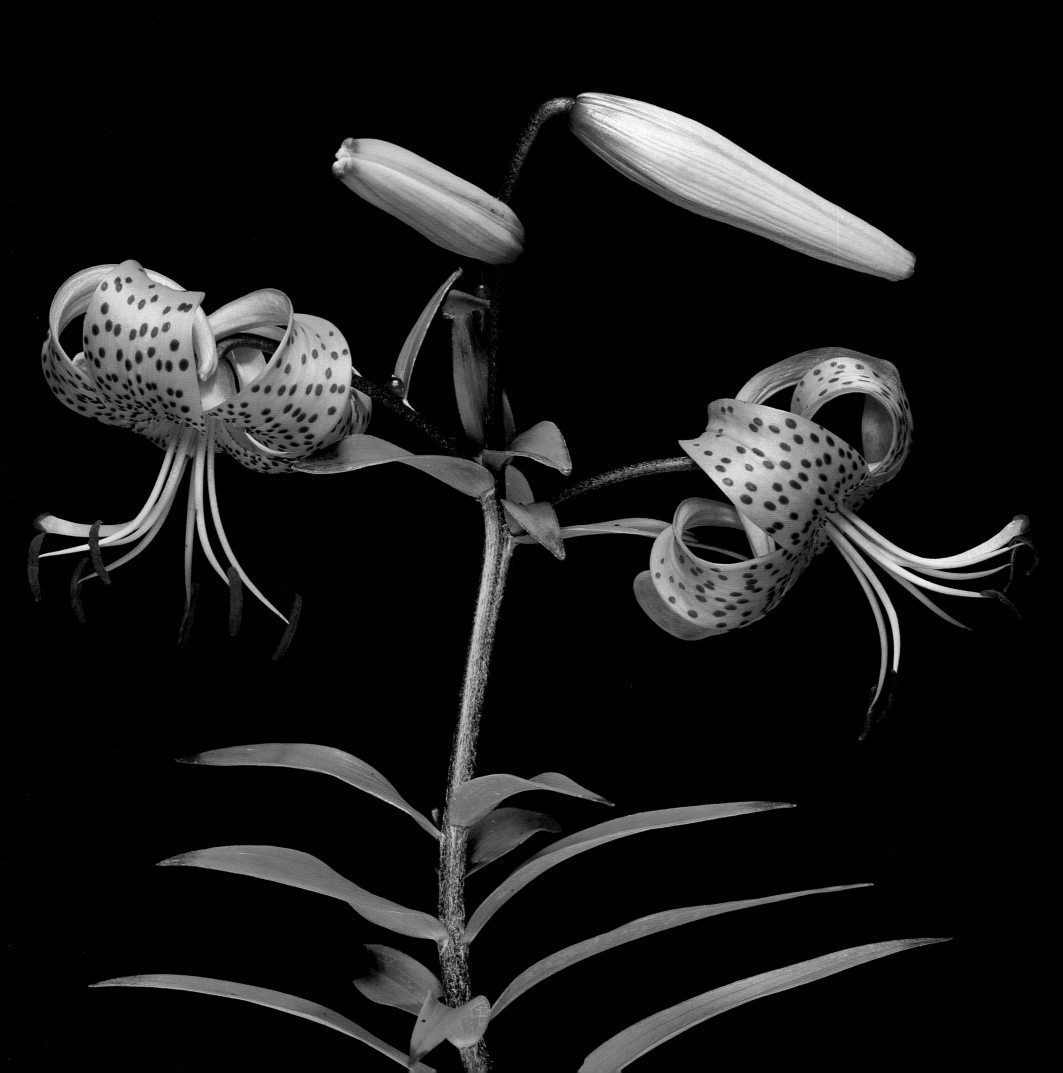

47 *(below) Dodecatheon pulchellum* 'Red wings'
(Shooting star)

48 *(right) Anacamptis pyramidalis*
(Pyramid orchid)

49 *(left) Nelumbo nucifera*
(Sacred lotus)

50 *(above) Amaryllis belladonna*
(Belladonna lily, Resurrection lily)

51 *(left) Tulipa acuminata* syn. *Amaria*
(Tulip)

52 *(right) Canna* 'Cleopatra'
(Indian shot)

53 *(below) Anthurium* 'Paradiso'

54 *(right) Hyacinthus orientalis*
(Hyacinth)

55 *(left) Clivia miniata*
(Kaffir lily)

56 *(above) Scadoxus puniceus* syn. *Haemanthus magnificus*
(Blood lily)

57 *(below) Cyclamen persicum*
(Sourbread)

58 *(right) Arum creticum*

59 *(left) Narcissus* 'Cantabile'
(Daffodil)

60 *(above) Meconopsis*
(Blue poppy)

61 *(below) Dahlia* 'Periton'

62 *(right) Schizostylis coccinea* 'Major'
(Crimson flag)

63 *(left)* *Galanthus* 'Magnet' (Snowdrop)

64 *(right)* *Eucharis amazonica* (Amazon lily)

65 *(below) Lilium longiflorum* 'Rosea'
(Easter lily)

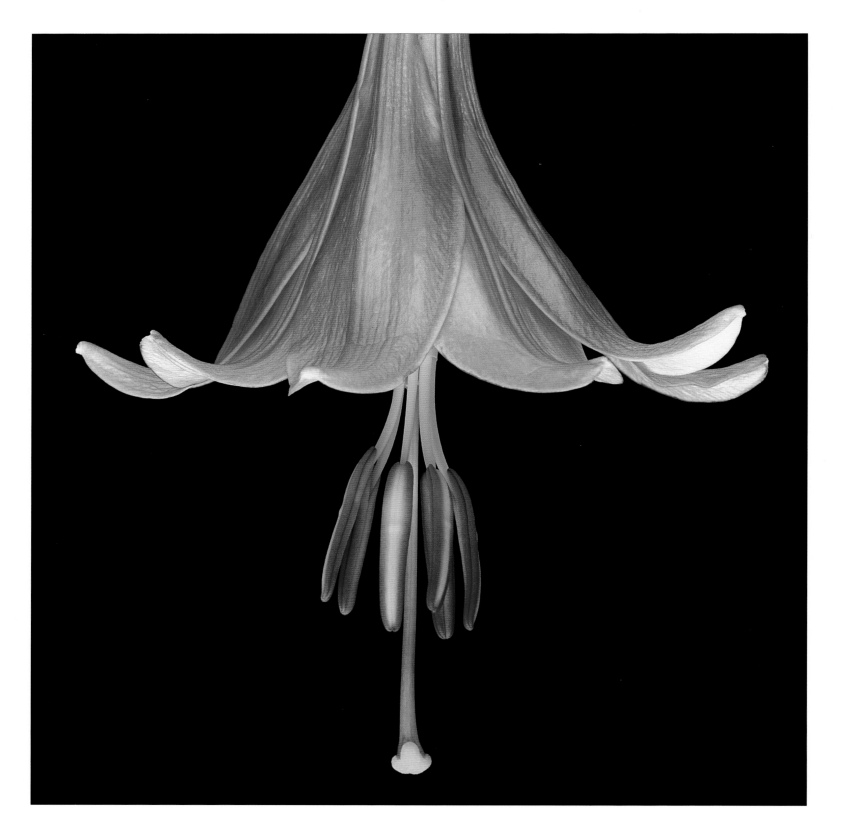

66 *(right) Disa uniflora*
(Orchid)

67 *(left) Lilium* 'Roma'
(Lily)

68 *(right) Iris* 'Early Light'

69 *(left) Curcuma alismatifolia*
(Tulip of Thailand)

70 *(above) Dicentra spectabilis*
(Bleeding heart, Lyre flower)

71 *(left) Hippeastrum* 'Romeo'
(Amaryllis)

72 *(above) Canna* 'Picasso'
(Indian shot)

73 *(below) Lilium longiflorum in bud*
(Easter lily)

74 *(right) Cymbidium* 'Pure Bisque'
(Orchid)

75 *(left) Muscari armeniacum* 'Blue spike'
(Grape hyacinth)

76 *(above) Anemone coronaria* 'de Caen'
(Peppy anemone)

77 *(below)* *Strelitzia reginae*
(Bird of paradise)

78 *(right)* *Hemerocallis* 'Ruffled Apricot'
(Daylily)

79 *(left) Trillium cuneatum*
syn. *Trillium sessile* of gardens
(Whippoorwill flower)

80 *(right) Fritillaria persica*

81 *(below) Erythronium* 'Pagoda'
(Dog's tooth violet)

82 *(right) Laeliocattleya* 'Susan Holguin'
(Orchid)

83 *(left) Begonia* 'Can-Can'

84 *(right) Fritillaria imperialis*
(Crown imperial)

85 *(below) Leucojum aestivum*
'Gravetye Giant'
(Summer snowflake)

86 *(right) Lilium longiflorum*
(Easter lily)

87 *(overleaf) Anemone pavonina*
(Windflower)

88 *(below) Begonia* 'Non Stop'

88 *(below) Begonia* 'Non Stop'

89 *(right) Iris bucharica*

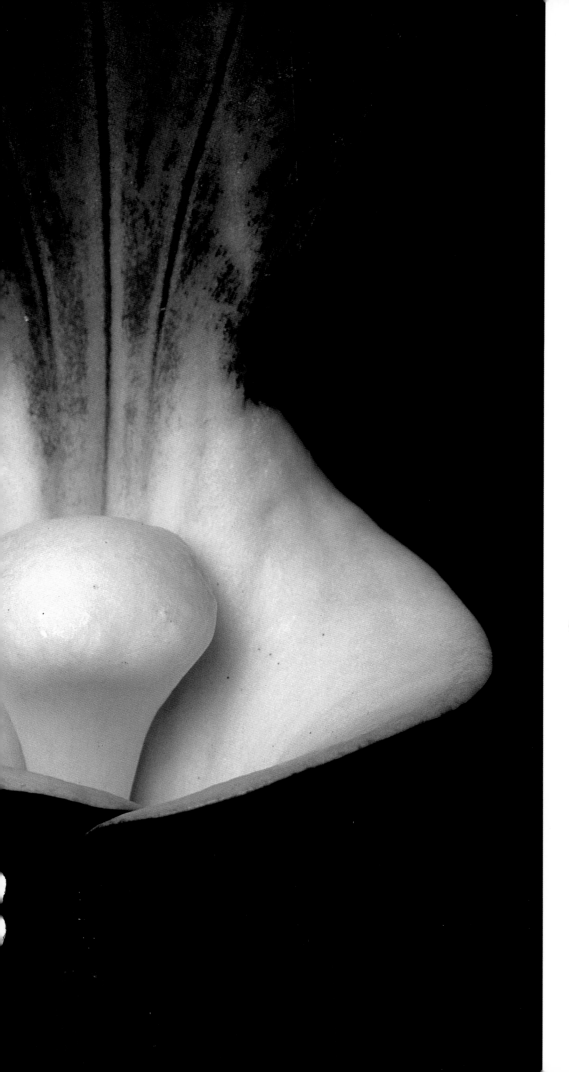

90 *(left) Arisaema sikokianum*

91 *(right) Sauromatum venosum*
(Monarch of the East, Voodoo lily)

92 *(below)* *Paeonia* 'Hyperion' hybrid
(Peony)

93 *(right)* *Alpinia purpurata*
(Red ginger)

94 *(left) Alstroemeria* ligtu hybrid
(Peruvian lily)

95 *(above) Cypripedium formosanum*
(Lady's slipper orchid)

96 *(below)* *Ornithogalum* hybrid

97 *(right)* *Narcissus* 'Merlin'
(Daffodil)

99 *(above) Ophrys apifera*
(Bee orchid)

BUYING BULBS

The main commercial market is focused on spring-flowering bulbs and in fall there is a big promotion of these "dormant" or "dry state" bulbs ready for planting. Most bulbs bought at nurseries and garden centers have been specially treated to protect them against insects and diseases, and also to ensure that they flower properly. Quality bulbs are essential for successful flowering, and it is important to check them before you buy.

Avoid bulbs showing any signs of disease, damage, or mold. And check that they are not soft or damp. Do not buy bulbs with spindly, white, or pale green shoots. Good quality bulbs are plump, firm, and heavy for their size. Check for a strong growth shoot. As a general rule, buy them as early in the season as possible when there is a good selection. Bulbs become damaged through constant handling or when kept in storage at garden centers or nurseries for long periods of time. In stores and supermarkets, warm conditions can lead to deterioration after just ten days.

Many bulbs are now sold prepackaged or by mail order. Apart from making a choice of variety and color, it is important to check the labels for the height of the plant, for planting and flowering times, and for cultivation tips. By careful planning, it is possible to extend the show of color. I usually take the trouble to make a quick plan of my borders, arranging the taller flowers at the back, and working systematically forward. I also take into account the flowering period and color. A handy tip is that some of the taller flowering bulbs such as lily tulips may require an infill of other plants to prevent them from being blown over in the wind.

Bulb size is very important. Although the actual size of different species varies greatly, a rule of thumb is that bulb size determines the quality of the plant and the size and quantity of the flowers. Good advice is to purchase the largest bulbs you can afford. Bulbs are measured by their circumference. Narcissus bulbs are sold not only by size but also by the number of bulb "noses." Some bulbous plants such as *Clivia* (kaffir lily), *Crocosmia* (falling star), and *Cyclamen* tend to be sold as leafy or flowering plants rather than as dry bulbs. Bulb offsets and undersized bulbs (measured by their circumference) are unlikely to flower the first season.

RIGHT: Narcissus

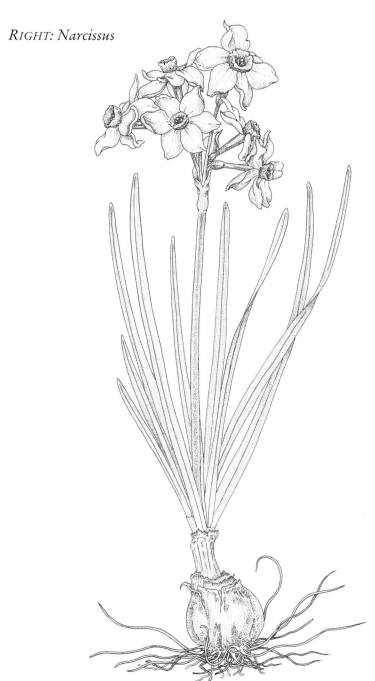

GENERAL CULTIVATION

The planting and aftercare of hardy bulbous plants is reasonably straightforward. Unlike shrubs, there is no thinning, pruning, or spraying to worry about. It is essential to decide where you are going to plant bulbs, taking into consideration their color, height, and flowering period. Certain varieties should be planted at different times of the year, and it is important to note the recommended time to plant. Plant only top-quality bulb stock, rejecting diseased or damaged bulbs. Remember, bulb size denotes the quality of the plant and flowers.

PREPARATION

Soil needs to be dug over about a week before planting. Nearly all bulbs require well-drained soil. If it is compacted or contains a high percentage of clay, mixing with coarse sand can loosen it. Dry peat or bonemeal can be added. The soil must not get waterlogged during winter months or bulbs will rot. Do not use fresh manure as a fertilizer.

PLANTING

Bulbs should be planted at a depth of about three and a half times their diameter. If the soil is sandy, they can be planted a little deeper, and if the soil is heavy, they can be placed slightly shallower. Plant bulbs as soon as possible after purchase, while they are still firm and without prominent shoots. Most true bulbs are ready to activate growth as soon as they are set into the ground. To stabilize themselves, they quickly develop roots from their bases. Stems then grow from the top of the bulb and probe upward through the soil. When they reach the surface, they are deactivated by their biological clock and stop growing. This is usually when winter weather sets in.

If planting in containers, free drainage is paramount. Make sure that drainage holes are sufficiently large and remain unblocked. Use shards to cover holes.

1 DIGGING THE HOLE

The width of the hole should be about twice the diameter of the bulb, and the base should be reasonably flat. The best tools to use are a trowel, a bulb planter, or a spade. If the soil is heavy, mix in a handful of coarse sand or peat in order to ensure that there is no air space between the base of the bulb and the bottom of the hole. Never put in fresh manure, as this will damage the bulb.

2 PLANTING THE BULB

Push the bulb firmly into the hole making sure that it is right side up: shoots to the top, roots to the bottom. Be careful not to damage the shoot or buds.

3 REPLACING THE SOIL

Use the dug-out soil to fill the hole evenly around the bulb and press down gently. Again, if the soil seems heavy, add peat or coarse sand. Rake the surface over and water the bulbs in if the weather has been dry. After bulbs have been planted, there will be no indication of their presence, so mark your plantings with a label. That way you will know what has been planted and you won't accidentally disturb the bulbs.

4 WATERING

Once the bulbs are planted and watered in, there is no need to water spring-flowering bulbs until just after flowering. If you water the ground above dormant bulbs during the winter, it will cause rotting. After flowering, it is a good idea to provide a little water until the time that the leaves fade and wither, as this encourages the bulbs and offshoots to develop.

5 FLOWERING

When the warmth of spring arrives, the shoots start growing again and produce flowers. The bulb supplies nourishment to support the growth of the plant. When the flowers fade, the plant should be deadheaded, leaving the stems and leaves intact. This strengthens the bulbs because energy is not wasted on producing seed. At this stage, the leaves replenish the food supply by photosynthesis and develop plant embryos in the bulbs for next year's flowers. By the time the leaves wither and die, bulbs have already fattened or been replaced by new ones.

6 Digging up Bulbs

Bulbous plants such as daffodils, crocuses, and fritillarias can be left in the ground to multiply and become more substantial. Most cultivated tulips and certain other bulbs should be dug up. Wait for the leaves to yellow and wither before cutting them off, allowing the bulb to build up nutrients for the next year's growth. Cultivated tulips produce their largest flowers the first spring after planting, and subsequently smaller bulbs are produced. When digging up the bulbs, taking care not to damage them.

7 Storing Bulbs

Cultivated bulbs require a period of dry and cool storage when they are dormant. Remove soil from the bulbs and discard any diseased or damaged ones. Sort into sizes and allow them to dry for a week or so. Store them in cardboard boxes, perhaps lined with newspaper to absorb any moisture. Do not store alongside apples because the bulbs can develop infection. Bulbs that don't have a tunic are best covered with peat or sand. The bulbs will stay dormant until the fall when the cycle is ready to start over again.

PESTS AND DISEASES

The same pests and diseases that attack other plants can affect bulbous plants, but prompt action will usually cure most problems. To prevent bulb rot and deter slugs, do not overwater. The most common pests are aphids, mealybugs, and scale, which mainly attack the stems and flowers. They are not usually a serious problem and can be treated by commercial remedies from a nursery, or by applying isopropyl alcohol on a cotton swab to the infected areas. Spring-flowering bulbs are fortunate because their flowering season ends before the aphids and leaf-eating caterpillars mature.

However, the underground bulbous parts are at risk at all times from numerous soil diseases and pests, as well as from animals and birds seeking food during winter months. One year I planted over two thousand tulip bulbs in a border adjoining a barley field. My garden was invaded by pheasants and only a dozen or so tulips bloomed that year.

RIGHT: Iris

PLANTING BULBS

FLOWER BEDS AND BORDERS

We are all familiar with the wonderful show of color in formal flowerbeds and borders, and this is the traditional method of planting. In spring, public parks and gardens can be a stunning and memorable sight. However, these displays are usually only temporary. When the flowers have died and the leaves have withered, the bulbs are removed so that the beds can be replanted with a colorful range of annual flowers. To give maximum effect, these public beds are often devoted to one or two varieties of bulbs, chosen for their stunning color. The formal effect can be dramatic, but for most private gardens it is best to choose several different varieties of bulbs, giving consideration to color, height, and the flowering period. This will give a far more attractive result.

Permanent planting is advantageous because it is not necessary to dig up the bulbs each year. They can be interspersed as an interesting addition to a mixed border or shrubbery, and they will flourish and multiply over the years. Surrounding plants can help to shelter and support tall growing bulbs and also hide the withered foliage at the end of the flowering season.

NATURALIZING BULBS

Naturalizing is a term used to describe a way of planting bulbs, usually in large open areas or under trees, to make them look as if they were native plants. This is not as simple to achieve as it may sound, and care should be taken to choose flowers that are not too large or too showy. When planting in grassy areas it is necessary to wait at least six weeks after flowering before the grass is cut. This gives the leaves time to produce nutrients that the bulbs need for the following year's growth. When selecting the bulbs, it is best to restrict your choice to just one or two varieties. This will give a more natural effect. Use a bulb planter for individual plantings. For an overall scheme, the turf can be lifted by cutting an "H" shape with a spade, then folding the layers back and planting the bulbs,

and finally replacing the turf. The classic technique is to scatter a handful of bulbs on the ground and to plant them where they land. Do not be tempted to make a geometrical design.

The same technique of scattering can be used effectively around the base of trees. However, some bulbs will not tolerate heavy shade, so use spring-flowering bulbs that will flower before the leaves of the tree mature.

BULBS FOR ROCK GARDENS

The basis of a rock garden is a sloping site utilizing a manmade outcrop of stones or boulders as the main feature. A weathered construction is very natural and appealing in any garden. When this feature is planted with flowers it immediately comes to life. A rock garden is an ideal environment for bulbous plants because the site is usually sloping and, therefore, free draining. With sandy or stony soil it will never get waterlogged. Rocks and boulders also offer delicate flowers protection against the elements. It is best to choose bulbs that flower in late fall, winter, or early spring. This is the time when many bulb species are in their prime, while other rock garden plants and shrubs are not. Select flowering bulbs with shorter stems: crocus, snowdrops, dwarf narcissus, dwarf iris, and other species in keeping with the rock garden's surrounding. It is also a good idea to choose hardy bulbs that can be left in the ground to spread, rather than those that need to be lifted each year.

Bulbs suitable for rock gardens are *Allium*, *Anemone*, *Colchicum*, *Crocus*, *Cyclamen*, *Fritillaria*, *Hyacinthella*, *Muscari*, *Narcissus*, *Puschkinia*, *Scilla*, *Trillium*, and *Tulipa* species.

BULBS IN CONTAINERS

In recent years there has been a container boom and nearly half the bulbs we buy nowadays are planted in containers. Most popular are the hardy spring-flowering bulbs such as snowdrops, crocuses, hyacinths, daffodils, and tulips. However, spring should not be the end of the season for bulb-filled containers because there are flow-ering bulbs suitable for the whole year. One drawback to bulbs purchased in containers is that the bulbs typically are cultivated for short-term bloom and display, thus their average life is shorter than that of bulbs sold for garden cultivation. Also, bulbs in containers rarely produce blooms the following year.

To overcome this problem you can fill the container with one type of bulb and after they have flowered, dig them up, discard them, and replace them with other plants. Alternatively, plant sev-eral layers of different bulbs that flower at consecutive times in order to extend the overall flowering period. Plan your container planting so as to combine bulbous plants such as daffodils, hyacinths, and tulips with perhaps ivy, pansies, and dwarf conifers.

It is important to incorporate a base layer of drainage. I use bro-

RIGHT: Crocus

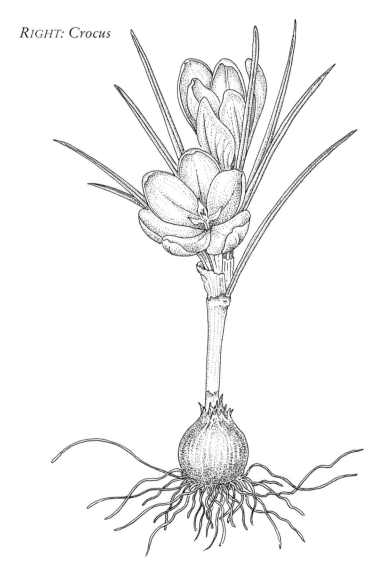

ken shards. Add a layer of peat, plant the bulbs, and then add fur-ther layers of potting compost and the bulbs, pressing down firmly around taller flowering bulbs.

GROWING BULBS IN GREENHOUSES

Hardy spring bulbs can be grown in an unheated greenhouse along with those flowers that require milder conditions. With a protected environment, one can expect outstanding plants and blooms.

If you are able to maintain temperatures so that they do not fall below 45 degrees Fahrenheit during the growth period, you will be able to grow a more comprehensive selection of flowering bulbs. Most are tender types that cannot tolerate frost conditions in win-ter and usually flower during the summer and fall months. These include *Amaryllis*, *Freesia*, *Nerine*, *Sparaxis,* and *Zephyranthes*.

To utilize the special heated conditions provided by the green-house, I am usually a little more adventurous and grow bulbs that require a warmer growing temperature of around 55 degrees Fahrenheit. These include *Achimenes*, *Canna*, *Clivia*, *Crinum*, *Gloriosa*, *Hippeastrum*, *Hymenocallis*, *Ornithogalum*, *Polianthes tuberosa*, *Sandersonia*, *Sprekelia*, and *Zantedeschia*. Tropical bul-bous plants and a few others require heated conditions of up to 65 degrees Fahrenheit.

BULBS IN THE HOME

Bulbs have become an important part of the houseplant market and different varieties are available to decorate the house virtually year-round.

Many half-hardy bulbs are now offered for sale as flowering houseplants with foliage rather than as dry bulbs. These include *Clivia*, *Eucharis*, and *Vallota*, and they generally retain their leaves and can be used for decoration all year round. However, the more common indoor plants such as *Amaryllis, Hippeastrum*, and *Narcissus*, lose their leaves after they have flowered. It is best to leave these in the pot and store them in a dry area until the foliage dies down, keeping the compost almost dry until the growth starts again the following season. With other bulbous plants such as tuber-ous begonias and calla lilies, it is advisable to lift them when the leaves have withered, and store the bulbs in peat, to await repotting the following season. Most flowering bulbs that are suitable for growing in pots and containers in the garden can also be brought into the house for display when they are in bud or flower. After flowering, either return them to the garden or discard the bulbs.

FORCING BULBS FOR INDOOR CULTIVATION

Forcing is the technique of encouraging plants to grow and bloom at an increased rate by artificial means. Many spring flowering bulbs can be tricked into flowering earlier than those cultivated in the garden. It is best to choose earlier flowering varieties such as *Crocus, Eranthis, Hyacinthus, Muscari, Narcissus,* and *Puschkinia.* Most tulips are not to be recommended because they become spindly; however, the dwarf varieties can make a bright and colorful display. Of the many bulb varieties available, be sure to choose those recommended for indoor flowering.

Use bulb fiber as a growing medium unless you intend to replant the bulbs in the garden, when a peat-based compost is best. Make sure you have adequate drainage. If you are using flowerpots, cover the base with shards. Put a layer of moist compost in the bottom of the container. Place the bulbs on it, making sure that they do not touch one another. Do not press the bulbs down too hard. Fill with more compost. The tips of the bulbs should just show above the surface. Press down and water lightly. Do not overwater.

These bulbs now require a cold, frost-free period in the dark, to simulate their natural dormant winter season. The ideal temperature is 40 degrees Fahrenheit. Put them in a black plastic bag and keep in a dark environment such as a shed or a garage for about eight to fourteen weeks, at which time shoots will start to emerge. When these are about one to two inches high, the containers can be brought indoors. Place containers in a shady position at first, and after a few days move nearer to a window. First the leaves will develop, then flower buds will follow within a couple of weeks. Position them for display in a bright, draft-free area, away from any artificial heat source.

For Christmas flowering, I plant bulbs in September and bring them into the light no later than early December. Specially treated bulbs for Christmas flowering can be purchased from garden centers where they are sold as "prepared bulbs," but they are significantly more expensive than regular bulbs. Treated bulbs and those "plunged" into darkness can also be made to flower in a receptacle containing only water as a nutrient, but these bulbs will not replenish and should be discarded after flowering.

BULBS AS CUT FLOWERS

Bulbous plants offer a colorful and varied selection of blooms for the enthusiastic flower arranger. Many varieties of cultivated narcissus, tulip, and hyacinth are available from our gardens in spring. In summer, they are followed by freesias, gladiolus, and lilies in all their splendor. Dahlias then brighten the shortening days of fall.

Cutting flowers does not harm the plants. However, do not remove the leaves because they are needed to replenish nutrients in the bulbs. Out-of-season flowers, which make arrangements more interesting, can be purchased from shops and at flower markets in all seasons. It never ceases to amaze me that cultivated tulips seem to be available throughout the whole year, and now the selection seems to be increasing annually. Flowers grown in your own garden will generally last much longer than cut flowers because commercial storage is inevitably detrimental to their longevity.

Cut flowers benefit from some treatment before display. For most plants, deep immersion in water is recommended. For bulbous flowers, only the stems should be immersed in a bucket of tepid water for two to eight hours while stored in a cool, dark area. In the case of hyacinths, narcissus, and tulips, it is necessary to cut away the base of the stems up to where the green starts because the white section is not capable of taking up water efficiently. Ranunculus and anemones can frustrate the flower arranger because the flowers and stems continuously bend toward the light source. Wiring the stems can easily resolve this tendency, although I personally find this trait a most attractive characteristic.

AUTHOR'S NOTE

My advice is for you to be adventurous, give a little extra thought to the bulbs you are planting, and enjoy the results!

PICTORIAL INDEX

Front cover: *Lilium* 'Bonfire'

Half-title: *Colchicum speciosum*

Frontispiece: *Crocus* 'Vernus white'

Dedication page: *Polygonatum* x hybridum

1 *Allium* 'Globemaster'

2 *Begonia* x *tuber hybrida* 'Double Picotee'

3 *Lilium* 'Marco Polo'

4 *Gloriosa superba* 'Rothschildiana'

5 *Heliconia rostrata*

6 *Arum creticum*

7 *Narcissus* 'Tête-à-tête'

8 *Roscoea auriculata*

9 *Nymphaea capensis*

10 *Begonia pendula* 'Double pink'

11 *Dahlia* 'Pearl of Heemstede'

12 *Sandersonia aurantiaca*

13 *Pleione forrestii*

14 *Gladiolus* 'Chloe'

15 *Iris* 'Chorus girl'

16 *Dicentra spectabilis f. alba*

17 *Convallaria majalis*

18 *Ranunculus asiaticus* 'Champagne'

19 *Cymbidium* 'Andre Ostobe'

20 *Tulipa* 'Balalaika'

21 *Nerine sarniensis*

22 *Fritillaria michailovskyi*

23 *Hermodactylus tuberosus*

24 *Anthurium andraenum*

25 *Crocosmia* 'Lucifer'

26 *Hyacinthoides hispanica*

27 *Iris pallida*

28 *Dodecatheon meadia alba*

29 *Zantedeschia aethiopica*

30 *Hippeastrum* 'Blossom Peacock'

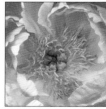

31 *Paeonia* 'Afterglow'

32 *Hemerocallis* hybrid

33 *Kniphofia*

34 *Ornithogalum arabicum*

35 *Arisaema tortuosum*

36 *Tulipa* 'Blue Parrot'

37 *Fritillaria meleagris*

38 *Trillium ovatum*

39 *Anemone blanda* 'White splendor'

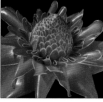

40 *Etlingera elatior*

41 *Anthurium scherzerianum* 'Rothschildianum'

42 *Arisaema candidissimum*

43 *Lilium* 'Le Rêve'

44 *Muscari armeniacum*

       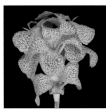

45 *Dahlia* 'Trengrove Jill'   46 *Lilium lancifolium*   47 *Dodecatheon pulchellum* 'Red wings'   48 *Anacamptis pyramidalis*   49 *Nelumbo nucifera*   50 *Amaryllis belladonna*   51 *Tulipa acuminata*   52 *Canna* 'Cleopatra'

53 *Anthurium* 'Paradiso'   54 *Hyacinthus orientalis*   55 *Clivia miniata*   56 *Scadoxus puniceus*   57 *Cyclamen persicum*   58 *Arum creticum*   59 *Narcissus* 'Cantabile'   60 *Mecanopsis*

    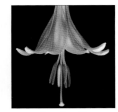   

61 *Dahlia* 'Periton'   62 *Schizostylis coccinea* 'Major'   63 *Galanthus* 'Magnet'   64 *Eucharis amazonica*   65 *Lilium longiflorum* 'Rosea'   66 *Disa uniflora*   67 *Lilium* 'Roma'   68 *Iris* 'Early Light'

 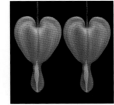      

69 *Curcuma alismatifolia*   70 *Dicentra spectabilis*   71 *Hippeastrum* 'Romeo'   72 *Canna* 'Picasso'   73 *Lilium longiflorum*   74 *Cymbidium* 'Pure Bisque'   75 *Muscari armeniacum* 'Blue spike'   76 *Anemone coronaria* 'de Caen'

77 *Strelitzia reginae*   78 *Hemerocallis* 'Ruffled Apricot'   79 *Trillium cuneatum*   80 *Fritillaria persica*   81 *Erythronium* 'Pagoda'   82 *Laeliocattleya* 'Susan Holguin'   83 *Begonia* 'Can-Can'   84 *Fritillaria imperialis*

     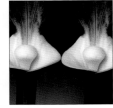  

85 *Leucojum aestivum* 'Gravetye Giant'   86 *Lilium longiflorum*   87 *Anemone pavonina*   88 *Begonia* 'Non Stop'   89 *Iris bucharica*   90 *Arisaema sikokianum*   91 *Sauromatum venosum*   92 *Paeonia* 'Hyperion' hybrid

93 *Alpinia purpurata*   94 *Alstroemeria ligtu* hybrid   95 *Cypripedium formosanum*   96 *Ornithogalum* hybrid   97 *Narcissus* 'Merlin'   98 *Dahlia* 'Anniversary Ball'   99 *Ophrys apifera*   Back cover: *Begonia* 'Double Picotee'

BULB SUPPLIERS

AMERICA

Amaryllis Bulb Company
Winter Haven, FL
Tel.: (800) 974-2558
www.amaryllis.com
Amaryllis bulbs

American Gardens
Indianapolis, IN
www.americangardens.com
Assorted bulbs online

Antonelli Brothers
Santa Cruz, CA
Tel.: (888) 423-4664
Begonia bulbs

B & D Lilies
Port Townsend, WA
Tel.: (360) 765-4341
www.bdlilies.com
Lily and daylily bulbs

Blooming Bulb Company
Medford, OR
Tel.: (800) 648-2852
www.bloomingbulb.com
Assorted bulbs

Breck's
Peoria, IL
Tel: (800) 722-9069
www.gardensolutions.com
Assorted bulbs, other plants

Burpee
Warminster, PA
Tel: (800) 888-1447
www.burpee.com
Assorted bulbs, other plants

Cascade Valley Farms
Parkdale,OR
Tel.: (888) 340-7098
www.cascadevalleyfarms.com
Assorted bulbs

Dirk Visser's Holland Bulbs
Ipswich, MA
Tel.: (800) 582-3650
www.dutchbulb.com
Dutch bulbs

Dutch Gardens
Adelphia, NJ
Tel: (800) 818-3861
www.dutchgardens.com
Dutch bulbs

Flowerbulb.com
Sassenheim, the Netherlands
US fax: (861) 760-0708
www.flowerbulb.com
Dutch bulbs online

French's Bulb Importers
Pittsfield, VT
Tel: (800) 286-8198
Assorted fall-blooming bulbs

Garden.com
Austin, TX
Tel.: (800) 466-8142
www.garden.com
Online garden shop

Geerlings Bulbs USA
Babylon, NY
www.dutchflowers.com
Dutch bulbs online

Harris Seeds
Rochester, NY
Tel: (800) 514-4441
www.harrisseeds.com
Assorted bulbs, other plants

Henry Field's Seed
Shenandoah, IA
Tel: (605) 665-4491
www.henryfields.com
Assorted bulbs, other plants

Holland Flower Company
Haarlem, the Netherlands
Fax: +31 23 5470833
www.hfc-flowerbulbs.nl
Dutch bulbs, ships
US/Can/Europe

Jackson & Perkins
Medford, OR
Tel: (800) 292-4769
www.jacksonandperkins.com
Assorted bulbs, other plants

John Scheepers, Inc.
Bantam, CT
Tel: (860) 567-0838
www.johnscheepers.com
Dutch bulbs

Jung Seed Co.
Randolph, WI
Tel: (800) 247-5864
www.jungseed.com
Assorted bulbs, other plants

Langeveld Bulb Company
Tel. (800) 526-0467
www.langeveld.com
Dutch bulbs online

Marlborough Greenhouses
Marlborough, NH
Tel.: (888) 822-6792
Assorted bulbs

McClure & Zimmerman
Friesland, WI
Tel: (800) 883-6998
www.mzbulb.com
Assorted bulbs

Netherland Bulb Company
Easton, PA 18045
Tel: (800) 788-8547
Assorted bulbs

New Holland Bulb Co.
Louisiana, MO
Tel: (888) 869-7300
Assorted bulbs

OHG Heirloom Bulbs
Ann Arbor, MI
Tel: (734) 995-1486
www.oldhousegardens.com
Heirloom, historic bulbs

Park Seed Co.
Greenwood, SC
Tel: (800) 845-3369
www.parkseed.com
Assorted bulbs, other plants

Rainbow Iris Farms
Bartlett, TX
Tel.: (512) 338-1618
http://rainbowfarms.net
Iris bulbs

Roozengaarde
Mount Vernon, WA
Tel: (800) 732-3266
www.roozengaarde.com
Assorted bulbs

Roris Gardens
Sacramento, CA
Tel: (916) 689-7460
Iris, bearded iris bulbs

Schipper & Company
Greenwich, CT
Tel: (888) TIP TOES
www.colorblends.com
Dutch bulbs

Schreiner's Gardens
Salem, OR
Tel: (800) 525-2367
www.schreinersiris.com
Iris bulbs

Spring Hill Nurseries
Tipp City, OH
Tel: (800) 544-0294
www.springhillnursery.com
Assorted bulbs, other plants

Van Bourgondien Brothers
Babylon, NY
Tel: (800) 622-9997
www.dutchbulbs.com
Assorted bulbs

Van Dyck's Flower Farms
Brightwaters, NY
Tel: (800) 248-2852
www.vandycks.com
Assorted bulbs

Van Engelen, Inc.
Bantam, CT
Tel: (860) 567-8734
www.vanengelen.com
Dutch bulbs

VWS
Brook op Langedijk, the Netherlands
Tel. +31 226-331050
www.vws-flowerbulbs.nl
Treated, "programmed" bulbs

Wayside Gardens
Hodges, SC
Tel: (800) 845-1124
www.waysidegardens.com
Assorted bulbs

White Flower Farm
Torrington, CT
Tel: (800) 503-9624
www.whiteflowerfarm.com
Assorted bulbs, other plants

Wild Blooms Plus
Wauwatosa, WI
Tel.: (877) 873-2085
www.wildbloomsplus.com
Bulb wholesaler

Wooden Shoe Bulbs
Woodburn, OR
Tel.: (800) 711-2006
www.woodenshoe.com
Dutch bulbs

AUSTRALIA
Broersen Seeds & Bulbs
365 Monbulk Road
Silvan, Victoria 3795

Lake Nurseries
439 Silvan Road
Monbulk, Victoria 3793
Tel.: (03) 9756-6157
www.global-garden.au/lake

Tesselaar's Bulb Nurseries
257 Monbulk Road
Silvan, Victoria 3705
Tel.: (03) 9737 9811
www.link.net.au/drt/pages/a
ttr29/welcome

Van Diemen Quality Bulbs
363 Lighthouse Cape
Wynyard, Tasmania 7325
Tel: +61-364-422-012

Windy Hill Flowers
Macclesfield Road
Monbulk, Victoria 3793

CANADA
Cannor Nursery
Victoria, British Columbia
Tel: (250) 658-5415
www.welovegardening.com
Asstd. bulbs, ships Canada

Cruickshank's Garden Guild
Toronto, Ontario
Tel: (800) 665-5605
Asstd. bulbs, ships Can./US

Dominion Seed House
Georgetown, Ontario
Tel: (800) 784-3037
www.dominion-seed-
house.com
Asstd. bulbs, ships Can./US

Eagle Lake Nurseries
Strathmore, Alberta
Tel: (403) 934-3622
Email: eglake@telusplanet.net
Asstd. bulbs, ships Canada

Gardenimport Inc.
Thornhill, Ontario
Tel: (800) 339-8314
www.gardenimport.com
Asstd. bulbs, ships Can/US

Horticlub
Laval, Quebec
Tel: (800) 784-3037
Fax: (800) 282-5746
www.dominion-seed-
house.com
Asstd. bulbs, ships Can/US

Lakeland Plant World
Dartmouth, Nova Scotia
Tel: (902) 435-1983
Asstd. bulbs, ships Canada

MacArthur's Nurseries
Moncton, New Brunswick
Tel: (506) 859-8999
Assorted bulbs, no shipping

McFayden Seed Co. Ltd.
Brandon, Manitoba
Tel: (204) 571-7520

Email: customerservice
@mcfaydens.com
Asstd. bulbs, ships Canada

Pan American Nursery
Surrey, British Columbia
Tel: (604) 576-8641
Email:
roses@pacificgroup.net
Asstd. bulbs, ships
worldwide

Paridon Horticulture Ltd.
Delta, British Columbia
Tel: (604) 596-3422
Email:hdejongh@paridon.com
Asstd. bulbs, ships
worldwide

Sheridan Nurseries
Dollard-des-Ormeaux,
Quebec
Tel: (514) 685-3640
www.sheridan-nurseries.com
Asstd. bulbs, ships
worldwide

Victoria Flower & Bulb
Victoria, British Columbia
Fax: (888) 768-BULB
www.islandnet.com/vicbulbs
Bulb warehouse

HOLLAND
Walter Blom & Zn.
Hyacintenlaan 2
2182 DE Hillegom

Frans Roozen B.V.
Vogelnzangseweg 49
2114 BB Vogelenzang

Van Turbergen B.V.
Achterwag 33
2161 DV Lisse

Fa. W.S. Warmenhoven
P.O. Box 221
2180 AE Hillegom

J.B. Wijs & Zn Zaadhandel
Binnenhof 46
1181 ZH Amstelveen

NORTHERN IRELAND
Knowehead
15 Ballynahatty Road,
Omagh
Co. Tyrone BT78 1PN

UNITED KINGDOM
Jacques Amand Ltd.
The Nurseries
Clamp Hill, Stanmore
Missx HA7 3JS

Avon Bulbs
Upper Westwood
Bradford-on-Avon
Wilts BA15 2AT

Jacques Bakker Holland
P.O. Box 111, Spalding
Lincs PE12 6EL

Walter Blom & Son Ltd.
Commbelands Nurseries
Leavesden, Watford
Herts WD2 7BH

Rupert Bowlby
Gatton, Reigate
Surrey RH20 0TA

Broadleigh Gardens
Barr House, Bishops Hull
Taunton, Somerset TA4 1AE

Cambridge Bulbs
40 Whittlesford Road
Newton, Cambridge CB2
5PH

P. de Jager & Sons Ltd.
The Nurseries, Marden
Kent TN12 9BP

Gee Tee Bulb Co. Ltd
Matmore Gate, Spalding
Lincs PE11 2PN

W.E. Ingwersen Ltd.
Birch Farm, Gravetye
Nr. East Grinstead
West Sussex RH19 4LE

Moolinaar Horti Group
Hoffleet Stow, Bicker
Boston, Lincs PE20 3AF

Paradise Centre
Twinstead Road, Lamarsh
Bures, Suffolk CO8 5EX

J. Parker (Dutch Bulbs)
452 Chester Road,
Old Trafford,
Manchester M16 9HL

Potterton & Martin
Cottage Nursery, Moortown
Road
Nettleton, Caistor,
Lincs LN7 6HX

O.A. Taylor & Sons Bulbs
Washway House Farm
Holbeach, Spalding,
Lincs PE12 7PP

Thompson & Morgan
London Road, Ipswich
Suffolk IP2 OBA

Van Tubergen UK Ltd.
Bressingham, Diss
Norfolk IP22 2AB

Wavex Pergola Ltd.
Anchor Road
Terrington St. Clements
Norfolk PE34 4HL

FESTIVALS

AMERICA
Daffodil Days
Bristol, RI
Tel.: (401) 253-2707
Annually in April.

Daffodil Festival
Sandwich, MA
Chamber of Commerce
Tel. (888) 33-CAPE-COD
Annually in April.

Pella, Iowa Tulip Time
Pella, Iowa
Tel: (515) 628-4311
Annually in May.
The town celebrates its
Dutch heritage with flower
shows, dutch dancing, and
evening parades.

Puyallup Valley Daffodil
Festival
Tacoma, WA
Tel.: (253) 627-6176
www.daffodilfestival.net
Annually in May.

Skagit Valley Gardens
"Tulips on Display"
Every day, 9 am–6 pm
Tel: (360) 424-6760
One acre show garden,
garden shopping, deli, fresh-
baked pies and breads.

Skagit Valley Tulip Festival
Mount Vernon, WA
Tel: (360) 428-5959
www.tulipfestival.org
Annually in April.
Tulip Transit offers bus
tours of the fields.

Tulip Festival
Orange City, IA
Chamber of Commerce
Tel: (712) 737-4510
Annually in May.
Dutch games, dancing, food,
costumes, wooden shoe
carving demonstration, and
live theater.

Tulip Time
Holland, MI
Tel: (800) 822-2770
www.tuliptime.org
Annually in May.
Special plantings of tulips in
streets and parks; exhibition
Dutch (*Klompen*) dancing;
parades and concerts.

AUSTRALIA
NOTE: In the Southern
Hemisphere the flowering
season is in September and
October.

Hobart Tulip Festival
Royal Botanical Gardens,
Hobart, Tasmania
Tel: (03) 6234 6299
Annually in October.
Fairs, shows, markets.

Tesselaar Tulip Festival
Silvan, Victoria
Tel.: +61 3 9737 9811
Annually from mid-
September to mid-October.
Organized by Tesselaar's,
whose garden and tulip farm
are open to the public.

Wynyard Tulip Festival
Wynyard, Tasmania
Tel: (03) 6442 3483
www.tased.edu.au/tasonline
/wyntulip
Annually in October.
Family entertainment
including working crafts
display, events on the river,
fireworks. Bus service to all
venues & tulip farm.

CANADA
Canadian Tulip Festival
Festival canadien des tulipes
Ottawa, Ontario
Tel: (613) 567-5757
Fax: (613) 567-6216
Tulip Hotline: (613) 567-
4447
www.tulipfestival.ca
Annually in May.
Tulip plantings and floral
displays.

Both the Royal Botanical
Gardens in Hamilton and
the Botanical Gardens in
Montreal have tulip displays
in the Spring.

HOLLAND
Floriade
Every 10 years (next 2002)
Venues vary
A "world's fair" of flower
growing, with themed
pavilions, reconstructed
gardens, and floral displays.

Tulip Festival
Bloemen Corso, Lisse
Annually in April/May.
Parade of decorated floats
and displays.

Tulip Festival
Keukenhof Gardens, Lisse
Annually in April/May
Parade of decorative floats
organized by Keukenhof
Gardens, who have a tulip
display in the Spring.

UNITED KINGDOM
Tulip Festival
Spalding, Lincolnshire
Annually in April/May.
Features a parade of
decorated floats along a
four-mile route, and floral
displays. Springfields
Gardens in Spalding have a
display of tulips every
spring.